karim
rashid

Plan.

Amorphic

eye sh...

Round bottom

karim
rashid

BY MARISA BARTOLUCCI
EDITED BY MARISA BARTOLUCCI + RAUL CABRA

CHRONICLE BOOKS
SAN FRANCISCO

Text copyright © 2004
by Marisa Bartolucci.

Design by Raul Cabra and Betty Ho
for Cabra Diseño, San Francisco.

Page 95 constitutes a continuation of
the copyright page.

Library of Congress Cataloging-
in-Publication Data available.

ISBN 0-8118-4208-8

Manufactured in China.

Distributed in Canada
by Raincoast Books
9050 Shaughnessy Street
Vancouver, British Columbia V6P 6E5

10 9 8 7 6 5 4 3 2 1

Chronicle Books LLC
85 Second Street
San Francisco, California 94105
www.chroniclebooks.com

COVER: BOW AND TUMMY HOLIDAY BAGS FOR ISSEY
MIYAKE, 1997
BACK COVER: CHESS SET AND SKETCH FOR BOZART TOYS,
2001
PAGE 1: GARBO GARBAGE CAN, 1996
PAGE 2: GARBO SKETCH
PAGE 3: GARBO AND GARBINO GARBAGE CAN FOR UMBRA,
1996
PAGE 6: KARIM RASHID, 2003

ABOVE: ARP 2 SIDE CHAIR, 1991

Acknowledgments

Thanks first go to Michael Regan, Karim Rashid's studio manager, whose good-humored help was essential to this book's creation. Thanks also go to Craig Miller for his learned insights, and to Bob Borden at Nambé and Paul Rowan at Umbra for their behind-the-scenes stories. Accolades go to Betty Ho once more for her intelligent design. And abounding gratitude is the reward of Alan Rapp at Chronicle Books for his steadfast support of this series.

Karim Rashid
Digital Avatar By Marisa Bartolucci

In the 1990s, if there had been no Karim Rashid, it would have been necessary to invent him. The Information Age was dawning; the New Economy was in foment; globalization was on the rise. And a new cultural matrix was emerging, defined by novel digital products and media—the Internet, cell phones, e-mail, laptops, portable DVD players—all commingling the real and the virtual. Its colonizers were a tribe of youthful beings, "global nomads," unfettered by antiquated notions of time, space, commerce, society, culture. They craved fresh products that spoke of their newly fluid, determinedly popular, suddenly affluent, boldly optimistic lives. Out of their ranks came a design avatar, Karim Rashid, a channeler of the Zeitgeist, fluent in state-of-the-art computer and manufacturing technologies, and a media-savvy sloganeer. With the creation of a colorful, inexpensive, sensuously shaped plastic trash can (an astounding three million and counting have been sold) and a dizzying number of other products, this toweringly tall, trendily attired, yet vaguely geeky designer set off a mini design revolution. His techno-organic objects, or "blobjects," as he calls them, became instant icons. In 2001, he issued a sumptuously produced, monograph/manifesto entitled *I Want to Change the World.* While some scoffed, no one laughed.

After September 11, 2001, the world did change. The New Economy was kaput; the ascendancy of globalization was in question. The optimism of a new millennium had turned to dust. It was now the dawning of the Age of Insecurity, and global nomads were cocooning. Karim Rashid might well have gone the way of many an IPO. Instead, new clients came thronging. **"After 9/11, people realized that no one is secure,"** **Rashid observes. "They needed to engage the moment, and that helped design. People became more savvy about material goods." It's a novel view, but a winning one for Rashid.**

Since 2001, he has designed more than two hundred new products, as well as two restaurants and three hotels. He has created numerous art objects, had two shows of his work at the avant-garde outpost Deitch Projects, *and* produced two CD compilations of electropop. Commercial success, it seems, has only burnished his vanguardist status. Even Bruce Sterling, that chronicler of the "future-today," has proclaimed Rashid "the prophet of a new and better way of life."

It would be hard to genetically engineer someone more suited for such a destiny. Rashid was born in Cairo in 1960 to an Egyptian father and a British mother, who met as art students in Rome and married while finishing their studies in Paris. Mahmoud Rashid, Karim's father, was the art director for Cairo Television. He and his wife, Joyce, already had a two-year-old son, Hani; a daughter, Soraya, would be born seven years later.

When the boys were still small, their parents decided that it would be better to raise them in Europe. After some years in Rome and then London, the family moved to Toronto, where Mahmoud Rashid took a position as set designer for the Canadian Broadcasting Corporation.

Moving so much made the family especially close; it also seems to have made them unusually open to change. Almost weekly Rashid's father would practice his craft by reconfiguring the family's furniture. Always creating, he would draw a pattern and sew up a new dress for his wife every Sunday. Karim served as his assistant. Because of these early dressmaking sessions, the young Karim first aspired to become a fashion designer.

Karim Rashid was a determined, resourceful boy. Soon after the family's move to Canada, Rashid told his mother he wanted to take up ice hockey. But she declined to buy him the requisite equipment. "You know he was so tall even then, I couldn't see him playing," she says. "I thought he could spend his time doing something more interesting." Her son would not be dissuaded. One day she came home and found that he had sewn his own outfit and protective pads. "What could I do? I went out and bought him a helmet," she says.

Rashid's eagerness to play hockey seems to have had more to do with fitting in than with any desire to play a rough sport in freezing temperatures. Most of the year allergies made outdoor activities a misery for him. He didn't miss communing with nature. "[It's] beautiful but excruciatingly dull, void of human intellect, human energy," he writes in his monograph. "We are nature, but we are creating a technological hypertrophic world."

Of the two brothers, Karim was the more playful—even flamboyant. A hopeless musician—"I failed at every instrument I tried"—he became a DJ in high school, playing a hybrid disco/punk. He attended his graduation in a pink satin suit he designed and sewed himself. "I had custom-made white leather boots that were more outrageous than anything Kiss ever wore," he boasts. Rashid also dyed his hair pink and painted his nails a matching hue. Fashion-forward attire has since become a trademark. For recent public appearances, he has donned a Dolce & Gabbana pink paisley velvet jacket worthy of Austin Powers and has clad his extremely large feet in white Prada shoes. The clothing business, as it happens, is in Rashid's blood. His maternal grandfather was one of the founders of Ian R. England, a venerable British textile company known for its worsted wool.

After high school, Karim attended Carleton University in Ottawa, where he studied industrial design. The program was largely informed by the pragmatic, functionalist philosophies of the Germans and Dutch. "Having been brought up by a painter, I kept wondering where's the poetry," remembers Rashid, who still considers himself an artist first and then a designer. He did not thrive in an environment where questioning premises was not encouraged. Nor was he interested in creating the kind of uniform products that came out of an engineering-driven design approach. Design, he thought, should be personal. His convictions did not impress his professors—he almost didn't receive his degree. Rashid was, nevertheless, getting a practical grounding in design. In his last year at the university, he took a full-time job with an Ottawa design firm, where he worked on telephony equipment. He learned not only how a product gets to market, but also how little design has to do with it.

The year after he graduated, he spent six months in Naples studying with two of the deities of modern Italian design, Ettore Sottsass and Gaetano Pesce. In the sixties, both men had been members of the Radical Architecture movement in Italy, comprising politicized young architects deeply ambivalent about postwar Italy's surging consumer culture and the banal products emerging from it. The only real outlet for their abundant talents was the design of those very products, since the political complexities of Italy's construction industry made it nearly impossible for them to participate in building desperately needed new housing. They confronted this dilemma by going beyond the functionalism of Bauhausian modernism to imbue everyday objects with meaning and individuality. Their endeavor blurred the boundaries between design and art, spurring such experimental groups as Archizoom, Studio Alchimia, and later, Memphis. By the early eighties, when Rashid would study with them, Sottsass and Pesce were beginning to probe the most pressing question within the profession: what should design be in a postindustrial age?

Rashid was captivated by the intellectual vigor and lively expression of Italian design, especially of these two men. After his graduate semester, he interned in the Milan-based industrial design studio of Rodolfo Bonetto in order to drink in the city's fabled design culture. It was a heady time. Still, the elitism of Italian design troubled him. "Anything interesting was for the high-end market," he says. "I was interested in creating products for everybody, in creating a 'designocracy.'"

While Italian designers have long collaborated with Italy's progressive furniture and tableware industries, their products are not truly mass-manufactured. Often, there is an element of skilled craftsmanship involved in the production, which makes them more expensive. The intellectual conceit behind much of their design often limits their audience as well. Trained to be pragmatic, Rashid found this Italian approach to industrial design ultimately unsatisfying. Not only wasn't it industrial enough, but it also avoided the tough realities of the commercial mass marketplace, the arena in which Rashid wanted to play.

Returning home to Toronto in 1984, Rashid got a job with KAN Industrial Designers, where he worked for such clients as Black & Decker and Samsung. Developing a snow shovel, a space heater, and a new post office box for Canada's postal service was hardly exhilarating work. Despite his impressive powers of persuasion when he made innovative proposals, such as producing a teakettle made with colored, clear-tint polypropylene, his clients responded with blank stares. (Some ten years later, Apple used this same plastic casing for its iMac, and the futuristic computers sold off the shelves.)

Rashid found an outlet for his creativity in Babel, a fashion company he founded in 1985 with two architect friends, Scott Cressman and Pauline Landriault. It was dedicated to designing clothing for one global culture. The label was written in fifteen different languages. The fashions were equally multiculti. One collection, for instance, blended details from the wardrobes of the

Mennonites and the Hasidim. "A few years later, Jean-Paul Gaultier showed almost the same thing," Rashid notes ruefully. But the *schmatte* business is a tough business; within a few years the company closed.

What makes Rashid unusual among his peers is that he seems equally captivated by issues of style and of industry. "I love roving trade fairs looking at new kinds of machinery, talking to production machine specifiers and industrial foremen," he says. "It's so inspiring when I see a great new machine. Sometimes I'll go to bed dreaming of what it can do."

His interest in new technologies made Rashid an early convert to computer-aided design (CAD). With this technology, designers can create three-dimensional images of highly complex conceptual objects so that they can analyze them and figure out their engineering before producing a prototype. This virtual prototyping makes product development more efficient and speedy, and so more cost-effective. In 1987 the software company Alias, a pioneer in the field, took offices next to KAN and invited Rashid to try out their product. He jumped at the chance. Before long he had convinced his employer to purchase computers for the KAN studio.

Rashid was equally interested in digital manufacturing. With the combined technologies of CAD and CNC (computer-numerical-controlled) machines, increasingly elaborate forms could now be mass-produced. Without these technologies, Frank Gehry would not have been able to so easily model the arching forms of the Guggenheim Bilbao nor calculate their complex engineering, much less fabricate the building's intricate titanium cladding cost-efficiently.

Rashid had begun teaching part-time in the late eighties as a way to balance the pragmatic side of his industrial design practice. In 1991, he moved to Providence, Rhode Island, to serve as an assistant professor at the Rhode Island School of Design. He took a theoretical approach to teaching. **"Design is taught as if it's about 'making.' The instruction borders more on craft,"** he says. **"I don't think design has anything to do with making. I wanted my students to think about issues concerning phenomenology, anthropology, commodity."** According to Rashid, this approach drew the ire of other professors, and his contract was terminated after the school year. He wasn't sorry. He hadn't been happy there. He found Providence a "decrepit town." And he thought RISD somewhat backward. He relates how when he arrived, six Silicon Graphic computers had been sitting in boxes in a basement—about a million dollars worth of equipment—for about six months. He was asked to set them up, because no one else in the department knew how. There was, however, one boon to his sojourn: an undergraduate painting major named Megan Lang. They fell in love, and married four years later.

Rashid was at a turning point. "I wanted to leave the profession," he says. "I was fed up." His brother convinced him to set up his own design studio in New York and seek out more challenging design jobs. A professor of architecture at Columbia University, Hani Rashid was becoming a leading researcher in the realm of digital architecture. By the end of the decade, his firm Asymptote would be on the architectural vanguard with its explorations into computer-generated architecture and the architectural hybridization of real and virtual space.

Rashid spent his first six weeks in the city sleeping on the floor of his brother's apartment. "Then I rented an apartment without a kitchen or shower. My 'design studio' consisted of a mattress on the floor and a Mac computer," he recalls. "It was hard, but I persevered." He pitched ideas to more than a hundred companies, targeting high-style European manufacturers as well as companies like Ethan Allen and La-Z-Boy. "Really awful icons of American manufacturing," Rashid calls them, whose image and products he offered to revamp for what he recognized was a dramatically changing marketplace. A new generation of furniture buyers, fans of MTV, Apple computers, and Nike sneakers, wasn't interested in the antique simulacra of their parents, yet the industry was ignoring this demographic taste shift. "These guys get so wrapped up in the production of what they make, they don't know what's happening," says Rashid. He met with manufacturers, but succeeded in capturing the interest of only one, Nambé, a little tableware company based in Santa Fe.

Nambé had been founded in 1951 to take advantage of a then high-tech material, an aluminum-based eight-metal alloy, developed at the labs at Los Alamos. It is an ideal material for tableware, lustrous as silver, but tarnish-free and temperature-retaining. Committed to contemporary design from its beginnings, Nambé used ancient sand-casting techniques to mold its special alloy into the kinds of biomorphic forms that would come to define mid-century American modernism. This aesthetic succeeded in distinguishing the company's products in a crowded marketplace, giving the firm impressive longevity.

In 1991, a new marketing director, Bob Borden, was brought in to expand the company's product line and its market base. "I wasn't interested in whether people over fifty liked Nambé," says Borden. "I was going after the twenty-five to thirty-five year olds." Borden was eager to develop a home accessories line—vases, votives, pepper mills, picture frames—that could be manufactured and sold at a competitive price yet possess a sensibility similar to Nambé's hand-crafted pieces. Borden looked for new design talent to help the company in this effort.

"Karim had no tabletop experience," he recalls. "But looking at his product designs I could see that he had a really good design language, and maybe more important, he could speak our design language." Rashid would be the first outside designer Borden commissioned to come up with ideas for the new line. With a few interns working on computers, Rashid elongated, squashed, and skewed the company's classic modern forms into technomorphic shapes. He proposed one hundred new designs. (To this day, his enthusiasm for new projects remains unbounded. "I work like a maniac," he admitted in an interview in the August 29, 2002, edition of the *Los Angeles Times.* "I have a tendency to do way too much.") Nambé decided to put thirty-three of the hundred into production.

Rashid became much more immersed in the development process than is usually the case with a designer, especially such a young one. When Nambé's executives went shopping for manufacturing equipment to produce the new line, Rashid accompanied them as an advisor. Later he spent time in the factory, figuring out the equipment's production possibilities with the foremen and operators. "It was a fantastic time," he says. "Interesting and difficult." He was especially interested in seeing how he could use this manufacturing technology to produce what he calls "digital craft."

In the early 1970s, Gaetano Pesce first championed the notion of the "industrial original." Reacting against what he saw as the soul-numbing uniformity of modernism and socialism, both reigning ideologies in Italy, Pesce conducted research into manufactured objects that would be individualized, not standardized by the production process. His experiments involved low-tech forms of manufacturing. In the nineties, Rashid wanted to create nonserialized objects using state-of-the-art serialized production. He called his idea "Variance," and he was so serious about its potential, he trademarked the term.

Variance™ was a way, he believed, that companies could reach niche markets. One of his first experiments involved a collection of podlike serving bowls, called Rainbow. By alternating the logarithms of the digitally controlled tool paths, he was able to manufacture bowls of variable heights and angled openings. But customers were confused when they got home and opened the box to find that the bowl inside wasn't identical to the one they had seen in the shop. A more commercially successful example of

Variance™ was a sugar and creamer set, called Jimmy. The two containers have differently angled tops, but identical bodies, so they can both be manufactured in one production run. Later, when Nambé expanded into crystalware, Rashid created a vase called Morph (1998), decorated with free-form bands of die cuts randomly altered by the computer, so the designs on each are different.

While Nambé was open to such experimentation, it wasn't in a position to market the notion of digital craft to consumers. "A company really has to have its own store to do something like what Levi's is trying to do with customized jeans," Rashid observes. Customers nevertheless responded to these designs, which possess "the hard sheen of crunched data," according to John Seabrook in a profile about Rashid in the September 17, 2001, edition of *The New Yorker*. Launched in 1995, Nambé's home accessories collection was a hit. With the help of Rashid's designs and those of other new designers, some suggested by him, the company has built a younger, hipper identity and is now developing its own line of stores.

Throughout the early nineties, Rashid offered design proposals to Umbra, a Toronto-based housewares company. "At first they would send back a letter with my designs. After a while, they just sent back the designs. It's easy to become disillusioned, but I kept going," he says. (In the telling of his rise to success, Rashid often comes across as a Horatio Alger hero, albeit one outfitted in gangsta glasses.) Eventually, he proposed some inexpensive trash cans with handles in translucent, acid pastel–hued virgin polypropylene. Umbra liked them. "They had beautiful forms, they could double as storage baskets, and their shape made them highly suitable for injection-molding," recalls Paul Rowan, the cofounder and vice-president of Umbra. Their rounded interiors especially impressed him, because they don't stick when the cans are stacked—which means paper doesn't have to be placed between the units for shipping, cutting costs. Umbra presented Rashid's designs to a focus group. Rashid's favorite, the Garbo, which featured a swooping rim, was the least liked. But Rowan and Umbra president Les Mandelbaum had a gut feeling and put it into production. The rest, of course, is industrial design history.

"That was a big hit, so they stuck with me," says the designer, who can alternate between endearing humility and childlike grandiosity. "I did a series of unsuccessful things after that [for Umbra], some brightly colored plastic bowls selling for only $3 or $4. They bombed. Timing is everything with these products. People weren't ready yet for plastic bowls." (Rashid notes his designs are typically three years ahead of popular taste. Sometimes more. "Companies are going into their archives and taking out old designs of mine," he says.)

He redeemed himself at Umbra a few years later with the Oh Chair, a sophisticated, digitized riff on the ubiquitous cheap plastic café chair. It sells for about $50, a bargain in the realm of designer goods. A CAD confection of curves and voids, offered in a delectable sampling of translucent pastels, the chair evinces the nerdy chic that once defined dotcom culture. The engineering of the chair was an extraordinary challenge, since its plastic body varies in thickness. Injection-molded objects usually have a skin with a consistent dimension. It took six months of experiments to get the right formula. The early chairs were so flexible that they could be turned inside out, but while this made them exceedingly comfortable, Rashid and the Umbra team worried that they would not support heavy bodies.

With a new polypropylene mix that would be stiffer, the long, nerve-wracking period of research and development paid off. Umbra has sold more than 500,000 chairs. They are especially popular in Europe. In the United States, says Rowan, a stackable plastic chair with a low price, no matter how trendy, still means a garden chair.

Rowan believes that one of the reasons Rashid's designs have been so successful is that "unlike other industrial design studios, Rashid and his team work with a design brief. I know other designers find him arrogant and a publicity hound, but I think he's a good collaborator. He's flexible. He's not a prima donna. He'll research the market, trends, brand positioning. He wants to make his product successful," Rowan says. "And Karim's personality is so important to the actual design. He has vision."

For Rashid, following a brief *and* injecting vision is what industrial design is all about. This willingness to work on industry's terms has prompted many design critics to compare him to the flamboyant Raymond Loewy, one of the pioneers of industrial design. Loewy called his formula for successful design "MAYA," an acronym for "most advanced, yet acceptable." It could, he said, keep "the customer happy, his client in the black, and the designer busy." Rashid has even higher expectations. "Good design," he says, "can help a company downsize and still grow. Because of the success of my designs, Umbra now has to produce less SKUs [stock-keeping units]." **In Rashid's hypothetical "rave new world" every product manufactured "would replace three." Multifunctionality is a dominant theme in his work. "Better objects edit the marketplace," he says. "Replacing the saturation of objects requires higher quality and new ideas."**

For Rashid, better objects are ones that are more visually and viscerally potent, yet it is not the form of the object that's important, according to one of his mantras, but the *experience* of the object. "Objects are lust," he writes in his monograph.

To understand how people experience objects, Rashid takes time to hang out in malls watching how consumers touch and examine the products for sale. When he designs an object, he tries to peel away its layers, like an onion, to get to its essential form. This approach has shaped his distinctive style, which he calls "sensualism," as the works are both sensual and minimal. Such forms provoke the most contemporary experiences says Rashid, "because 'soft' means human, friendly, approachable, and comfortable."

This stripping away to the essential is something Loewy also tried to do in the thirties as one of the leading proponents of streamlining. A design style largely concocted by the advertising world to represent a smooth, high-speed, optimistic vision of the machine-age future, it had enormous appeal. The reason, explained Loewy, was that it "symbolizes simplicity—eliminates cluttering detail and answers a subconscious yearning for the polished, orderly essential." Something similar might be said for Karim Rashid's sensualism.

Today, there are no better media for mass-producing such forms than polymers. And Rashid is their poet. Synthetic rubber, Santoprene, Evoprene, polyolefins, and silicones prickle the designer's imagination with their protean potential, their ability to mold into marvelously sensuous, otherworldly forms, to take on a gorgeously hued translucence or a sleek metallic sheen, to imitate the inviting silkiness of skin. Rashid has shown a masterful ability to play with these qualities throughout his work, but especially in his packaging design. Indeed, some consider this his forte. "I like his Prada packaging, because it's all about waste and consumerism, and that's what Karim is best at—it's an ideal marriage of his talent and a product," opined a nameless pundit in the New Yorker profile. "He has a great talent for the ephemeral."

Unlike many designers, Rashid has no problem with ephemerality. He embraces it as emblematic of our times. "If you are not part of the 'now,' you are not really alive," he says. In early middle age, he remains an enthusiast of youth culture, a composer of technopop, a wearer of tattoos. Images from his personal vocabulary of digitized symbols encircle his upper arm and that of his wife. **If Rashid could change the world, all the objects you own would be replaced every five years. "Every object would have to be perfectly cyclical as not to collect waste," he explains with a nod to environmentalists. "Generations would not be able to pass down anything in its original form . . . The idea of antiquity would be a simulation."**

Some of his most innovative packaging has been for Issey Miyake. He met the fashion designer in 1996 at an exhibition of Rashid's furniture at the Tokyo gallery, IDÉE. Impressed by what he saw, Miyake asked Rashid to create shopping bags for his boutiques. Rashid proposed creating a plastic shopping bag that would be so striking it could be used in Miyake's shops not just for a season, but for several years. He argued it would be terrific branding because customers could reuse the bag as a chic carryall.

A year later, Miyake had put several of Rashid's shopping containers into production. Perhaps the most ingenious was Torso. It shipped as a die-cut sheet of translucent polypropylene and sat on the store counter in a stack until a customer made a purchase. Then the salesperson neatly folded the plastic into a torso-shaped bag, hence the name. A sheet of co-injected polyethelene, each side a different fluorescent shade, was inserted into the floor of the bag, imbuing the bottom half with a mysterious glow. As the plastic was translucent, the garment was visible in the bag. Rashid's designs became must-haves for fashionistas, many of whom would buy the least expensive item in the store to get a bag. Miyake also sold Rashid-designed polypropylene purses, which customers bought as a flat sheet and went home and folded into a handbag.

Rashid has since gone on to design some seventy pieces of packaging for Miyake's fragrance line. The best of this collection may be the two-in-one travel kit he designed in 1999. It consists of a blue square plastic bottle for deodorant, banded on three sides by an angled, U-shaped, milky-toned plastic bottle for eau de toilette. Both containers are made of a specially concocted polypropylene—which makes the design revolutionary, since the chemical components of plastic usually break down when exposed to the chemicals in the fragrance, discoloring the container and affecting the scent. The design of the dual containers is also extraordinary, because the kind of injection blow-molding used in the manufacture works best with curved forms. It took much patient engineering and experimentation for Rashid and the production team to get the design right. The fit of the containers is perfect; they even slip apart for separate use. Call it packaging as art.

Some designers take this equation for granted, for Rashid it is a cause. Method, a San Francisco–based maker of stylishly packaged home cleaners and deodorizers, commissioned him in 2002 to conceive a dispenser for an upscale dishwashing detergent, available in four different scents. "It's the project I'd been waiting for all my life," says Rashid with earnest rapture. "It was a chance to put a piece of sculpture on every American's kitchen sink."

As Rashid saw it, there were two main problems with detergent dispensers: the pull-top got gunky and the bottles had awful-looking labels. These dispensers had always offended Rashid and many of his aesthetic-minded friends, who would hide them under the sink. Rashid realized such problems could be resolved simply by turning the dispenser on its head. The Method version has an appealing bloblike form—bulbous top, narrow middle, and conical bottom—that fits comfortably in the hand like a pepper mill. To dispense the soap, you simply squeeze—it pours out of a specially engineered self-closing valve at the bottom. The product's

name and information is printed directly on the bottle in a stylish Metro font. The stores where it has been test marketed can't keep it on the shelves.

Karim Rashid is now the design director for Method. He's excited that the company is a startup, founded by two twenty-somethings. "An e-commerce shakeup is going to happen in the bricks and mortar businesses," he asserts. And Rashid wants to be part of the quake. He thinks that world needs a revolution. He's still frustrated by it. He estimates that the ratio of designs he creates to actual products is at a disheartening fifty to one. Whole lines of products have never gone beyond the prototype phase because the companies that commissioned them were ultimately too nervous to produce such radically rethought objects.

Still, Rashid *is* altering worlds, at least environments. Since 2000, he has begun to branch out into interior design—restaurant and retail interiors, hotels. The

jewel among these projects is the Hotel Semiramis in Athens, owned by Greek industrialist and art collector Dakas Joannou. Rashid has designed everything right down to the "the glass you gargle with and the disposable bathing suit . . . It's a little like 'Being Karim Rashid,'" he jokes. But he insists the physical details are not as important as the experience he's creating. While most boutique hotels attempt to give visitors a tangible sense of place, Rashid has sought to immerse them in a realm of virtuality. He likens it to the movie *Tron.* When he came back from a visit to a room mock-up in the spring of 2003, he couldn't contain his excitement. "I felt like I was inside a computer. It had that energy, that connectedness to the world," he says.

To simulate the experience of being a digital avatar, Rashid has stripped the hotel of familiar references. Guests will find no main desk for check-in, no room numbers—each door will have a unique symbol, fifty-five in all. Guests will receive a special wand, which when waved, will open their room's door, safe, and mini bar. A Jenny Holzer–like, guest-controlled board with tracking LED running in front of each room's doorway will broadcast information: "It could be 'Do not disturb,'" says Rashid, "or guerilla propaganda." In any case, material and immaterial worlds will merge. The Semiramis will surely be trippy enough to pack some now cocooning global nomads onto Athens-bound planes.

Ever persevering, Rashid is producing digital craft, not for the mass market, but the art market. In 2002, at New York's Sandra Gering Gallery, he showed plastic objects called Mutablobs, representing various moments in the computer-generated evolution of a technomorphic form that grew, twisted, and finally wrapped back into itself. At different intervals in its digital development, data was sent to a rapid robotic prototyping machine and was transformed into a physical object. These technomorphic forms also served as the compositional subjects for a series of four digital paintings authored by Rashid. In both series the data used in their creation was destroyed, so the objects and paintings can never be exactly replicated, making them originals of a sort. The show sold out.

Artist, designer, businessman, Rashid's roles are constantly morphing. And that, for Rashid, is what freedom is all about. **"If freedom were a form it would be a never-ending undulating boundless biomorphic shape in perpetual motion," he writes in his monograph. "Form follows fluid."** But will Rashid's creativity be boundless? Will his work stand the test of time? Such are the questions being asked by critics about this design phenomenon now in mid-career. "When designers don't slow down, they don't have time to think and grow," observes R. Craig Miller, the design curator for the Denver Art Museum. "Karim is on such an incredible roll right now, he needs to always remember to give himself that creative time as a designer."

At present, Karim Rashid's place in design history remains fluid.

Since 2001, Rashid has designed more than two hundred new products, as well as two restaurants and three hotels. He has created numerous art objects, had two shows of his work at the avant-garde outpost Deitch Projects, *and* produced two CD compilations of electropop. . . . Even Bruce Sterling, that chronicler of the "future-today," has proclaimed Rashid "the prophet of a new and better way of life."

 Karim Rashid ponders a new creation, 1998. The chair, lamp and table are his designs.

✛ FAR LEFT: Kissing vases for
Nambé, 1995

✛ ABOVE (FROM LEFT TO RIGHT):
Flare, Striker, Kismet, and Blossom
salt and pepper collection for
Nambé, 1995

✛ MIDDLE LEFT: Kissing salt and
pepper shakers for Nambé, 1995

✛ LEFT: Tuscany pepper mill for
Nambé, 1996

✛ ABOVE: Jimmy sugar and creamer for Nambé, 1995

✛ ABOVE BACKGROUND: Detail of Freestyle carpet for Directional, 2000

✛ RIGHT: Morph vase for Nambé, 1998

✛ FAR RIGHT: Linea vase for Nambé, 1998

 Industrial martini glass for
Bombay Sapphire, 2000

 New Move glassware: Blob, Spoo, and Dive for Leonardo, 1999

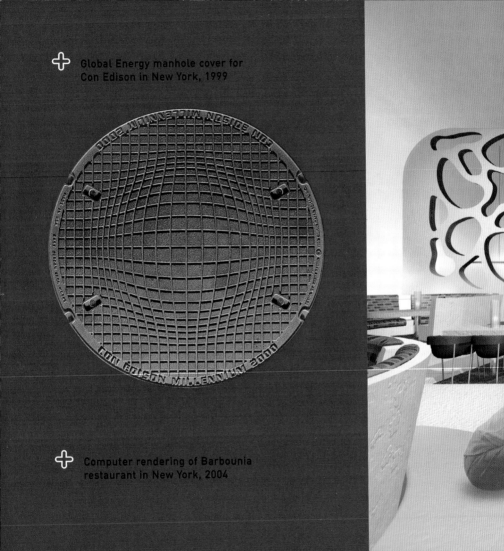

Global Energy manhole cover for
Con Edison in New York, 1999

Computer rendering of Barbounia
restaurant in New York, 2004

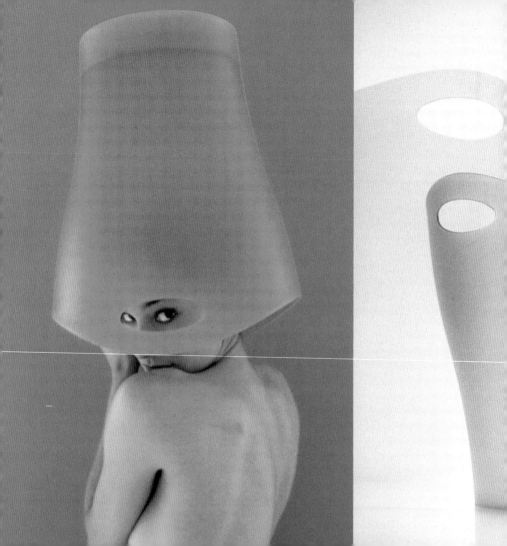

 PREVIOUS PAGES: Garbo and Garbino garbage cans for Umbra, 1996

 Wowowo sofa for Galerkin Furniture, 1999

 Spline Chair for Frighetto, 2001

 FOLLOWING PAGES: Pleasurescape
exhibited at Rice Gallery in Houston,
2001

LEFT TO RIGHT: Soft Collection
table lamp, Shroom table lamps,
and Undule pendant lamp for
George Kovacs Lighting, 1999

FOLLOWING PAGES: (LEFT)
Soft Collection pendant lamp for
George Kovacs Lighting, 1999

FOLLOWING PAGES: (RIGHT)
Computer rendering of hotel room
at the Hotel Semiramis, Athens,
2001

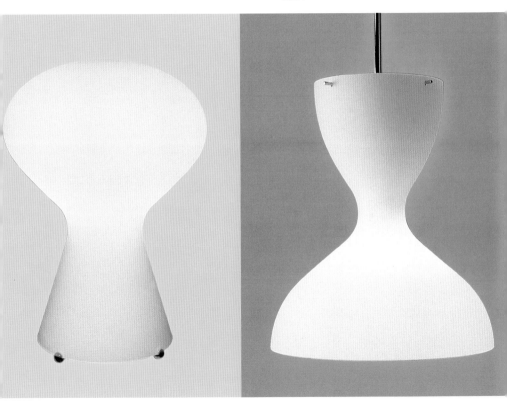

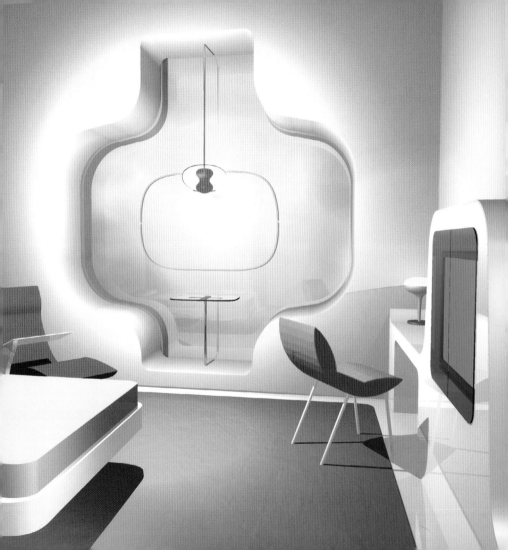

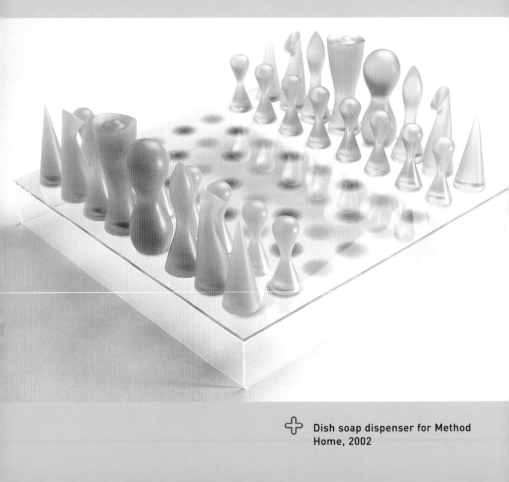

✛ Chess set for Bozart Toys, 2001

✛ Dish soap dispenser for Method Home, 2002

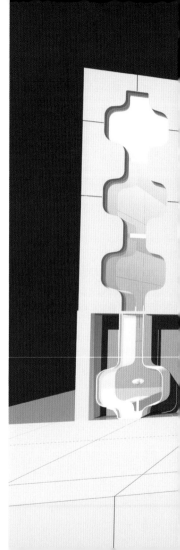

✚ Ribbon desktop landscape for
Totem, 1999

✚ Computer rendering of exterior
facade of the Semiramis Hotel,
Athens, 2001

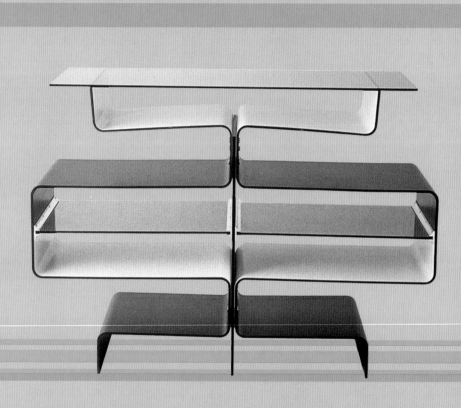

✛ RAD16 table for Decola Vita
Furniture Collection, IDÉE, 1998

✛ Coffy table, for Decola Vita
Furniture Collection, IDÉE, 1999

A new generation of furniture buyers, fans of MTV, Apple computers, and Nike sneakers, wasn't interested in the antique simulacra of their parents.

✛ FOLLOWING PAGES (LEFT): FloGlo 1 & 2 chairs for IDÉE, 1997

✛ FOLLOWING PAGES: (RIGHT): Wedji stools for for Decola Vita Furniture Collection, IDÉE, 1998

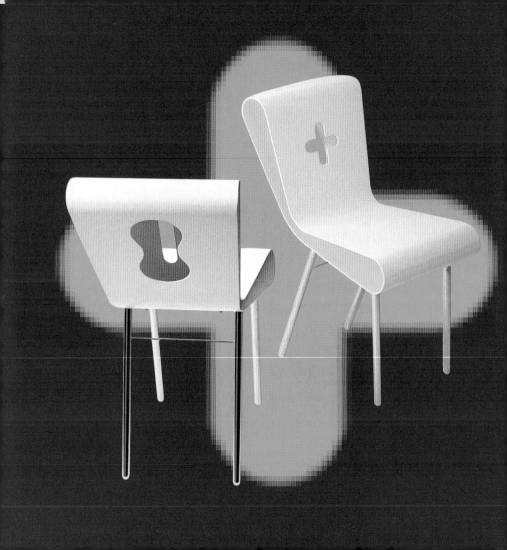

✛ Karim with Loungin chair (for IDÉE, 1996) and carpets (for Directional, 2000)

✛ Mousepad Collection for Totem, 1999

Syntax stacking chair for Decola
Vita Furniture Collection, IDÉE,
1998

Asym chair for Decola Vita
Furniture Collection, IDÉE, 1998

✛ FOLLOWING PAGES: Momo100Pink,
100-seat sofa for Belgian Biennale,
Durlet, 2000, and later exhibited at
Deitch Projects in New York, 2001

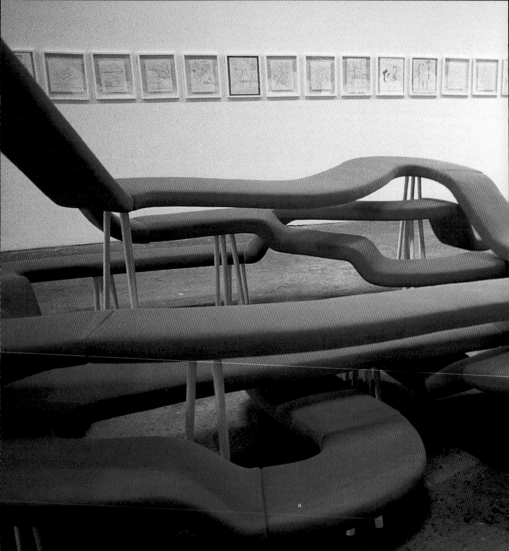

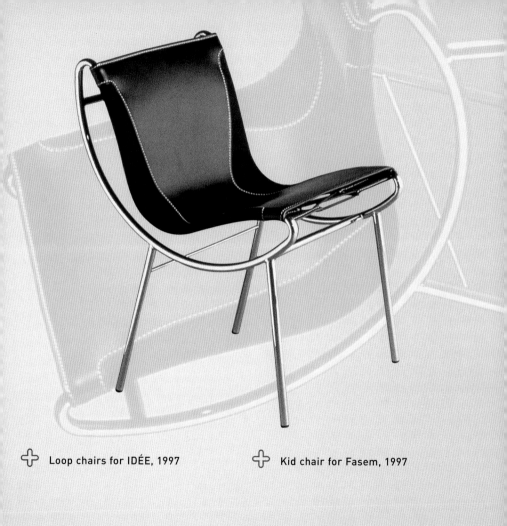

⊹ Loop chairs for IDÉE, 1997

⊹ Kid chair for Fasem, 1997

✚ Aphex chairs for IDÉE, 1997

✚ Morimoto Restaurant for Starr
Enterprise in Philadelphia, 2001

The engineering of the chair was an extraordinary challenge, since its plastic body varies in thickness. Injection-molded objects usually have a skin with consistent dimension.

✛ Oh Chair for Umbra, 1999

✛ FOLLOWING PAGES: Oh Chairs, and injection molded tables for the cafeteria at the Sendi Mediatheque building by Toyo Ito, Japan, 2000

5 Senses objects for
Sandra Gering Gallery
in New York, 1998

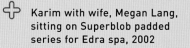

Karim with wife, Megan Lang,
sitting on Superblob padded
series for Edra spa, 2002

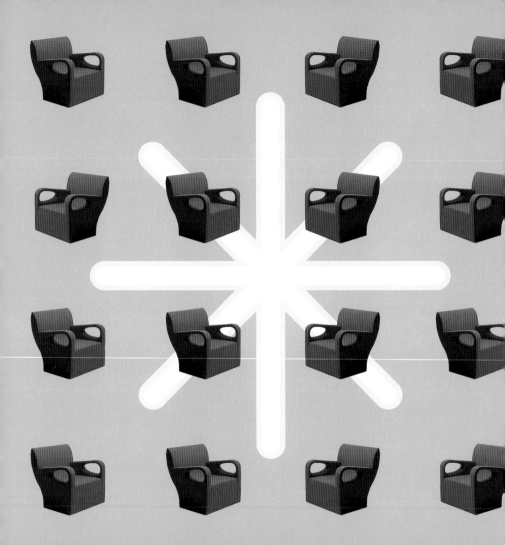

✛ Arp arm chair for IDÉE, 1996   ✛ Arp 3 Couch for IDÉE, 1996

✛ FOLLOWING PAGES: (LEFT)
Computer rendering of hotel room
at myhotel Brighton

✛ FOLLOWING PAGES: (RIGHT)
Swing chair for Frighetto, 2001

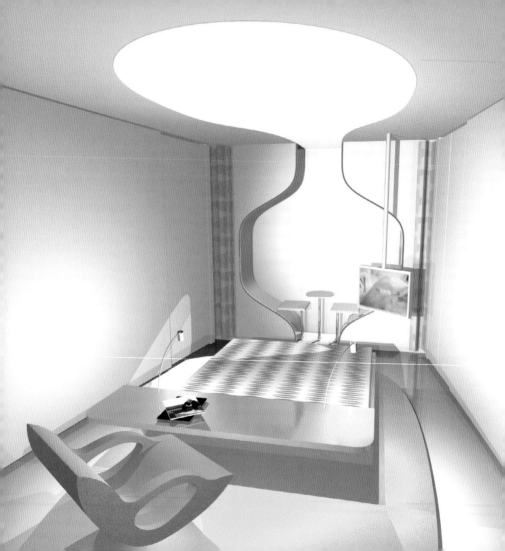

Synthetic rubber, Santoprene, Evoprene, polyolefins, and silicones prickle Rashid's imagination with their protean potential, their ability to mold into marvelously sensuous, otherworldly forms, to take on a gorgeously hued translucence or a sleek metallic sheen, to imitate the inviting silkiness of skin. Rashid has shown a masterful ability to play with these qualities throughout his work, but especially in his packaging design.

PREVIOUS PAGES: Plob interactive
environment for Capp Street
Project in San Francisco, 2001

 Karim (left) with his brother Hani
Rashid

 Stratascape, designed with Hani
Rashid and Lisa Anne Couture of
Asymptote, Philadelphia, 2001–02

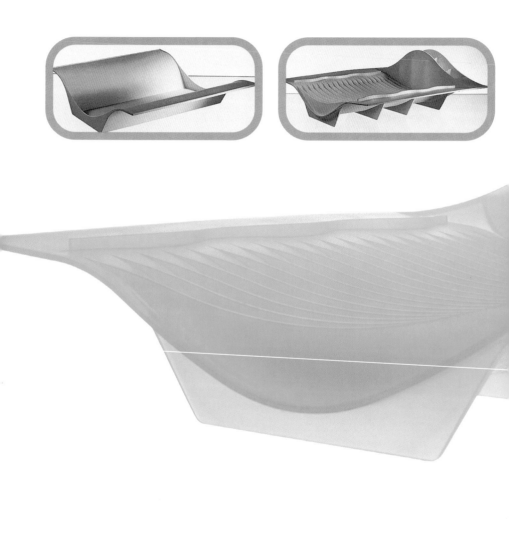

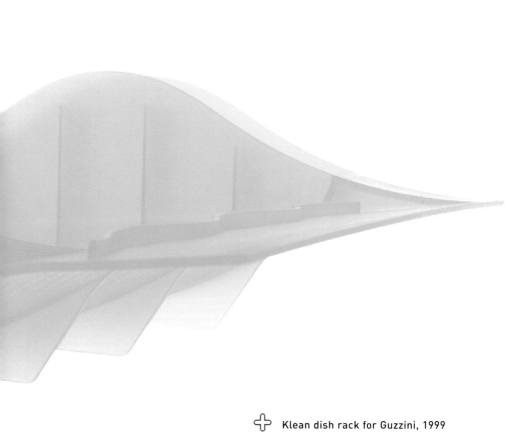

Klean dish rack for Guzzini, 1999

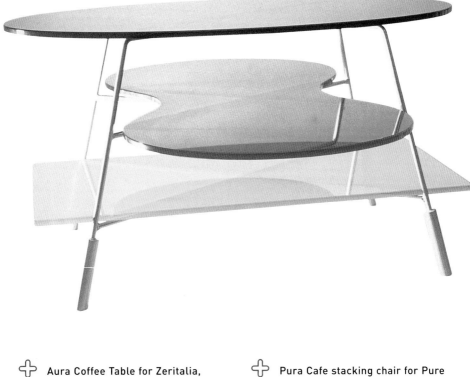

✚ Aura Coffee Table for Zeritalia, 1997

✚ Pura Cafe stacking chair for Pure Design, 1998

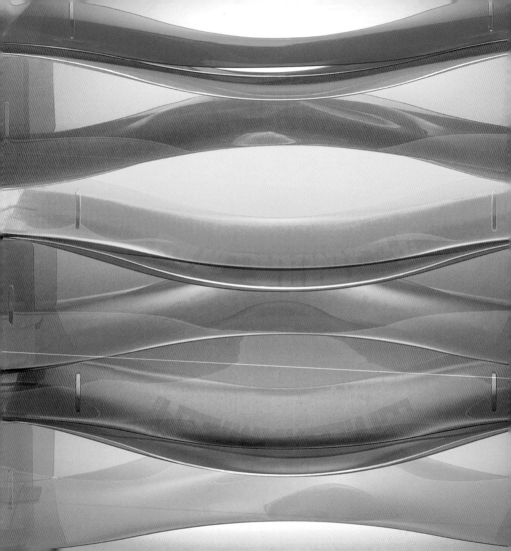

 Bow and Tummy holiday bags for Issey Miyake, 1997

 FOLLOWING PAGES: (LEFT AND RIGHT) Torso and Bust bags for Issey Miyake, 1997

DEODORANT SANS ALCOOL
ALCOHOL FREE DEODORANT

EAU DE
TOILETTE

Rashid has since gone on to design some seventy pieces of packaging for Miyake's fragrance line. The best of this collection may be the two-in-one travel kit he designed in 1999. It consists of a blue square plastic bottle for deodorant, banded on three sides by an angled, U-shaped, milky-toned plastic bottle for eau de toilette. Both containers are made of a specially concocted polypropylene—which makes the design revolutionary, since the chemical components of plastic usually break down when exposed to the chemicals in the fragrance, discoloring the container and affecting the scent.

✚ 2-in-1 travel kit, L'eau D'Issey Pour Hommes, eau de toilette and alcohol-free deodorant for Issey Miyake, 1999

✚ FOLLOWING PAGES: Prada unidose and multidose containers/packaging for Prada Skin Care Line, 2000

**Reviving Concentrate/
Hand
Concentré Revivifiant/
Mains**

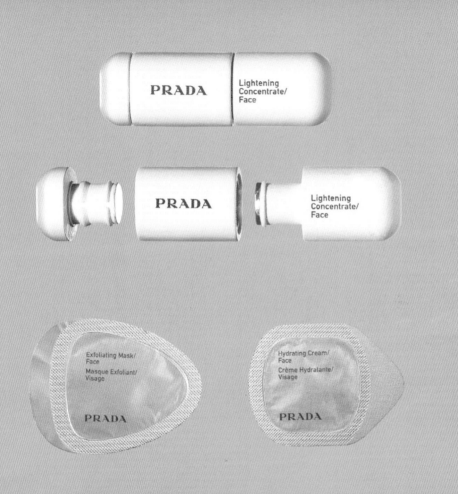

e capsule, produced
nd exhibited at the
Museum of Art, 2000

Member's Party, Going Forth by Day, at the Guggenheim Museum, New York, 2002

FOLLOWING PAGE: Karim being interviewed by a Norwegian TV crew while attending the Innotown Design Conference in Alesund, Norway, 2002

KARIM RASHID BIOGRAPHY

1960 Born on September 18 in Cairo

1967 Moves with family to Toronto from London

1982 Graduates from Carleton University in Ottawa with a BA in industrial design. Spends six months in Naples pursuing graduate design studies with Ettore Sottsass and Gaetano Pesce.

1983 Intern in the office of the industrial designer Rodolfo Bonetto in Milan

1984 Goes to work for KAN Industrial Designers in Toronto, where he designs products for such companies as Black & Decker and Samsung. Founds Babel, a clothing company, with two architect friends, Scott Cressman and Pauline Landriault.

1991 Leaves KAN; accepts position as assistant professor at the Rhode Island School of Design in Providence

1993 Moves to New York City and founds his own design practice

1995 Creates extensive range of products for Nambé's new manufactured home collection; marries painter Megan Lang

1996 Designs the Garbo trash can for Umbra

1998 His collection of Decola Vita furniture is exhibited at IDÉE, Tokyo; Pure Rashid show at Totem Gallery, New York City

1999 Designs the Oh Chair for Umbra. Awarded Daimler Chrysler 1999 Award; George Nelson Award, the Silver IDEA Award, and the Philadelphia Museum of Art Collaboration Award. Commissioned by Con Edison to design a commemorative millennium manhole cover for New York City's streets.

2000 First gallery show at Deitch Projects, New York City

2001 Produces *I Want to Change the World,* a monograph/manifesto with Universe Publishing

KARIM RASHID BIOGRAPHY (CONTINUED)

2002   Designs Method's inverted dispenser for dish soap

2003   Designs the first Nambé shop in Denver; it receives Store of the Year Award from
            National Association of Store Fixture Manufacturers. Releases two CDs *newyorkelec-
            tronew* and *newyorkelectropunkfunk* on Neverstop Music.

PHOTO CREDITS

Albion Associates, Inc.
pp. 36–37

Ron Amstutz
pp. 66 (all), 67

Chris Barnes
p. 17 (bowls)

David Bashaw
p. 17 (top), 28 (vases)

Antoine Bootz
back cover, p. 44

Fabrice Bouquet
pp. 21 (top), 86

CCAC Watis Institute for Contemporary Arts
pp. 74–75

Jürgen Frank
pp. 24–25

Lynton Gardiner
pp. 40 (all), 41 (all), 42

Doug Hall
pp. 3, 17 (garbo), 35

Francis Hammond
pp. 80, 81

Yoshiharu Kondo
pp. 48, 51, 51–55, 58, 60, 70, 71

Steven Krause
p. 53

Toby McFarlan Pond
pp. 88–89

Peter Medilek
p. 46

Courtesy of Karim Rashid Studio
cover (bags), 1, 2, 4, 11 (all), 17 (vase and chair), 21 (soap), 26 (all), 27, 28 (carpet), 29, 30, 31, 33, 34, 37, 38–39, 39 (right), 43, 45, 47, 49, 50, 52, 54, 56–57, 57 (all), 59, 61, 62, 63, 64, 65, 68, 72, 73, 76 (small), 78, (top two renderings), 82, 83, 84, 85, 90 (left), 92

Ilan Rubin
pp. 32, 78–79

Emil Tremolada
p. 69

Chi Chi Ubin
pp. 90 (right), 91

Adam Wallacavage
pp. 76–77

George Whiteside
cover (portrait), p. 6

INDEX